Which detail doesn't fit? Which painting is it from? ....

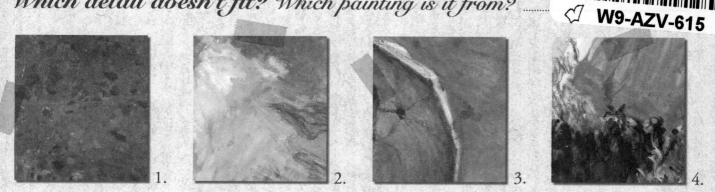

1.   2.   3.   4.

What's this scribble?
To find out, shade in black the areas with a black dot. How many times can you see this shape ⊚ ?

5.   6.

Hello

You are the artist!
You can colour each
one of these paintings.
If you prefer, the details
are easier to shade.

*Here's a trick
if you don't have
any palette!*

*Mix your colours on a
piece of cardboard or
on a sheet of paper. Find
out the same colours that
are on the painting.*

**The colour pencils
on each page**
show the main colours
of the painting.
If some areas are white,
just don't shade them.
You can also use paint
or felt pens.

*I have just spent the
day outdoors, painting.
The light was superb!
I set up four can-
vases in front of
a scene I
painted this winter.
It's so tiring painting
the light – it keeps changing! Still, I think these
pictures will come
out quite nicely,
even if I started out*

feeling rather dispirited. Yesterday, I started a study of some apple trees. When I went back, someone had picked all the apples! So I threw away the canvases... See you soon.

Monet.

They say I am an "Impressionist" because I paint my impressions - the wind in the trees, the smell of poppies, the quiet of a pond...These impressions never last long, so I have to get the paint on the canvas really fast!

What a curious boat! I turned it into a floating studio so I could get even closer to the endlessly changing reflections of my garden in the water...

Poppies at Argenteuil

**Railway excursions
are all the rage…**
*Now city people can take the
train and enjoy the countryside.*

Artists, too, are moving outdoors
*to paint in the open air, and in all weathers too!
In the old days, we had to make our own colours
in the studio. Now they come in tubes, ready to use!*

My favourite model
*is my son… young Jean.
Can you find him in my paintings?
He's often there. Here he's with his mother.*

Pure colours…
*Look at the red of the poppies.
For the petals, I dabbed on quick little
touches of paint with my brush.*

P..

W ....

Woman with a Parasol

It's a windy day!
I can feel it, can you? Look closely: the scarf is blowing, so is the dress, and the grass is rippling. Even the clouds seem to be zipping along. Poor Suzanne must be shivering!

What colour is light?
I treat light as if it were a colour on my palette.

Something familiar here!
Well yes, I painted two pictures like this. In the other one, Suzanne is looking to the right.

Is it a portrait or a landscape?
Well, we can't see Suzanne's face. What we see is the wind and light around her. I painted this picture as if it were a landscape.

The Japanese bridge, green harmony

"Four seasons" on the Japanese bridge
I am in my garden at Giverny, in my floating studio.
I am going to paint this pond. All right, I painted it yesterday
too, but the weather was different then. So I'm starting again.
Some people call me "the painter of weather"!

The water isn't blue…
It's all green! Everything is merging
into everything else: leaves, waterlilies
and reflections. Without the bridge,
you wouldn't know where you were.

T ....

....

Waterlilies, in the morning

Where's the bridge?
In the other pictures I painted the Japanese bridge, the banks and the trees. Here, I am looking only at the water.

The canvas is full of water!
It's trivial because this painting measures more than 12 metres long.

As the days go by…
All I paint now are the reflections of my garden in the pond. Everything is mixing together, more and more. My eyes hurt. I can't see very well anymore.

At the end of my life, I am making "huge" paintings and yet they were made in front of this tiny little pond!

What's a waterlily?

- ✒️ a fish which lives in a bath tub
- ✒️ a white flower which grows in my pond
- ✂️ a swimming instructor who teaches in a pond

The quiz
Circle the right answer

I am an "Impressionist" because

- ✏️ I impress all my friends
- ✒️ paint my feelings, my impressions
- ✂️ I have the impression that I'm dumb

The woman with the parasol

- ✒️ Is called Suzanne
- ✂️ Is called Suzette
- ✏️ Is called "Peau d'Âne"

My son Jean

- ✒️ Is my favourite model
- ✂️ Is my opponent when we play ping-pong
- ✏️ Is my best friend

I paint something which won't last for long

- ✂️ Such as chocolate cake
- ✏️ Such as a clock
- ✒️ Such as cloud

To paint water

- ✒️ I sit on my boat
- ✏️ I take a bath
- ✂️ I wait for a storm

Some say that I'm the "art of meteorology" because

- ✒️ I often paint the 4 seasons
- ✏️ I paint frogs
- ✂️ I often paint weather reports

Total: ✏️ ☐ ✂️ ☐ ✒️ ☐

I use light

- ✏️ To see better
- ✂️ To enlighten my paintings
- ✒️ As if it were a colour

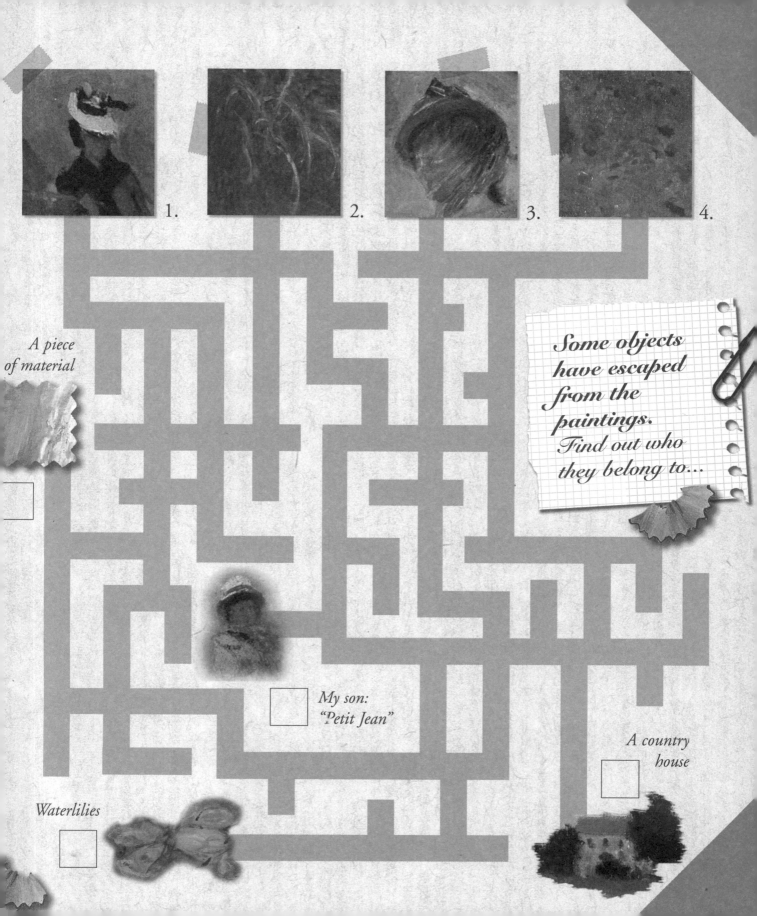

1.

2.

3.

4.

A piece
of material

*Some objects
have escaped
from the
paintings.
Find out who
they belong to...*

My son:
"Petit Jean"

A country
house

Waterlilies

In a drawer I found these weird images... Do you recognize them?

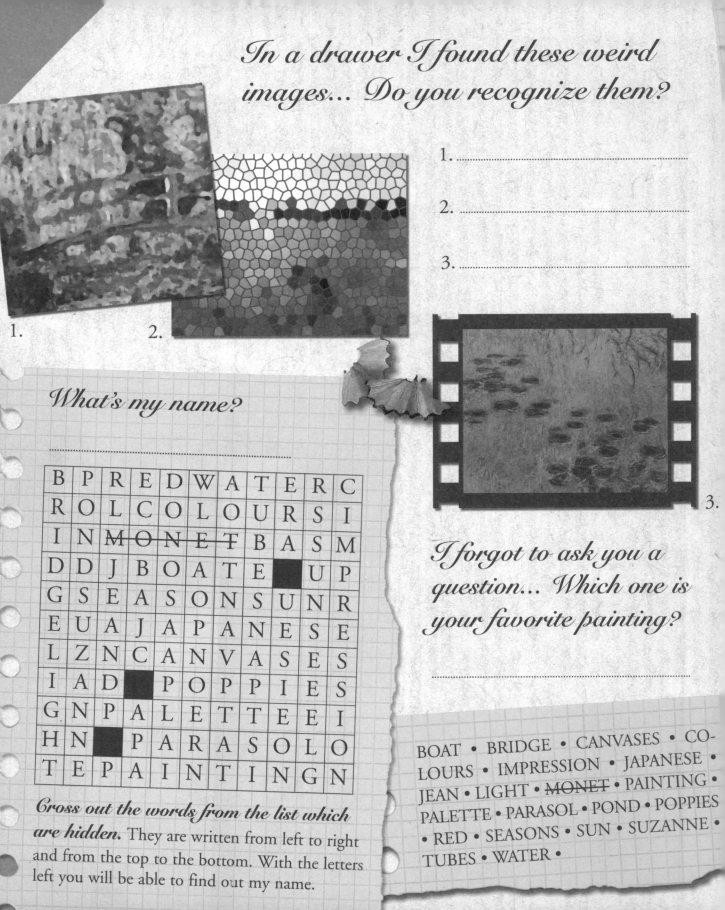

1. ....

2. ....

3. ....

1.

2.

3.

What's my name?

....

B	P	R	E	D	W	A	T	E	R	C
R	O	L	C	O	L	O	U	R	S	I
I	N	M̶	O̶	N̶	E̶	T̶	B	A	S	M
D	D	J	B	O	A	T	E	■	U	P
G	S	E	A	S	O	N	S	U	N	R
E	U	A	J	A	P	A	N	E	S	E
L	Z	N	C	A	N	V	A	S	E	S
I	A	D	■	P	O	P	P	I	E	S
G	N	P	A	L	E	T	T	E	E	I
H	N	■	P	A	R	A	S	O	L	O
T	E	P	A	I	N	T	I	N	G	N

Cross out the words from the list which are hidden. They are written from left to right and from the top to the bottom. With the letters left you will be able to find out my name.

I forgot to ask you a question... Which one is your favorite painting?

....

BOAT • BRIDGE • CANVASES • CO-LOURS • IMPRESSION • JAPANESE • JEAN • LIGHT • M̶O̶N̶E̶T̶ • PAINTING • PALETTE • PARASOL • POND • POPPIES • RED • SEASONS • SUN • SUZANNE • TUBES • WATER •

Solutions / answers

Don't forget to sum up the points!

| | / 9 |

The scribble
enables to see Monet's signature.
There are 9 ⊚ in the drawing.

| | / 7 |

The 7 differences
are circled in red on the picture.

| | / 3 |

The odd one: Jean disappeared from the field of poppies

| | / 6 |

Which detail doesn't fit?
Detail n° 1 doesn't belong to the painting.

Total points | / 25 |

**Woman with
a Parasol (1886)**
The Orsay Museum, Paris

**The odd one out
of the 6 pictures**

**Poppies
at Argenteuil (1873)**
The Orsay Museum, Paris

**The Japanese bridge,
green harmony (1899)**
The Orsay Museum, Paris

**Waterlilies, in the
morning (1916-1926)**
Musée de l'Orangerie, Paris

My name is Claude !

B	P	R	E	D	W	A	T	E	R	C	C
R	O	L	C	O	L	O	U	R	S	I	I
I	N	M	O	N	E	T	B	A	S	M	
D	D	J	B	O	A	T	E	U	P		
G	S	E	A	S	O	N	S	U	N	R	
E	U	A	J	A	P	A	N	E	S	E	
L	Z	N	C	A	N	V	A	S	E	S	
I	A	D		P	O	P	P	I	E	S	
G	N	P	A	L	E	T	T	E	E		
H	N		P	A	R	A	S	O	L	O	
T	E	P	A	I	N	T	I	N	G	N	

The weird images are...

The Japanese bridge, green harmony (n°1), Poppies at Argenteuil (n°2), Waterlilies, in the morning (n°3).

Des détails se sont échappés des tableaux. Retrouve les propriétaires...

1. 2. 3. 4.

Un tissu ensoleillé

[3]

Des nymphéas

[2]

[1] Mon fils : Petit Jean

Une maison à la campagne

[4]

True ☐ False ☐

I made huge paintings in front of a tiny little pond

Monet
painted in 1874
by Edouard Manet

The lost objects
This is the road we should have taken.   / 4

The quiz: All of the good answers are the ↪ You can find some information about the answers on the pages where the paintings are reproduced.   / 8

True / False   / 3
It's true!

Total points   / 15

+

Total points from the other page   / 25

=   / 40

Au clair de ma plume

Design and text: Raphaëlle Aubert.

© Published by Au clair de ma plume 2012. Law no. 49956 of 16/07/49 concerning publications for young people. Graphics system: José Vilela. Printed in May 2012 by Escourbiac in Graulhet. Registration of copyright: October 2008.

www.auclairdemaplume.com